101
RESOLUTIONS
FOR THE
NEW YEAR

101

RESOLUTIONS

FOR THE

NEW YEAR

NANCY WALKER HALE

BARBOUR
PUBLISHING

New Year, New You

Each new year ushers in a time of renewal, reevaulation, and resolution. But sometimes it's difficult to see the things that we can change to better ourselves and the lives of people around us. *101 Resolutions for the New Year* offers specific ideas grounded in God's Word that can change your everyday life. Each resolution is accompanied by a Bible verse that reaffirms the importance of the action or attitude change. It's the perfect kick-start you need for the new year!

The Editors

1

I will forget my troubles and put on a smile.

*Give all your worries to Him
because He cares for you.*
1 PETER 5:7 NLV

2

I will take a break from the stresses of life.

"Are you tired? Worn out?
Burned out on religion? Come to me.
Get away with me and you'll recover your life.
I'll show you how to take a real rest.
Walk with me and work with me—
watch how I do it.
Learn the unforced rhythms of grace.
I won't lay anything heavy
or ill-fitting on you.
Keep company with me
and you'll learn to live freely and lightly."
MATTHEW 11:28 MSG

3

I will give to a
worthwhile charity.

*Pure religion and undefiled before
God and the Father is this,
To visit the fatherless and widows
in their affliction, and to keep himself
unspotted from the world.*
JAMES 1:27 KJV

4

I will get in touch with an old friend.

Perfume and incense bring joy to the heart,
and the pleasantness of one's friend
springs from his earnest counsel.
PROVERBS 27:9 NIV

5

I will end gossip when it reaches me.

Fire goes out without wood,
and quarrels disappear
when gossip stops.
PROVERBS 26:20 NLT

6

I will take the first step in restoring a relationship.

Live creatively, friends. If someone falls into sin, forgivingly restore him, saving your critical comments for yourself. You might be needing forgiveness before the day's out. Stoop down and reach out to those who are oppressed. Share their burdens, and so complete Christ's law. If you think you are too good for that, you are badly deceived.

GALATIANS 6:1–3 MSG

1

I will celebrate life.

*The man who does not give up
when tests come is happy.
After the test is over,
he will receive the crown of life.
God has promised this to
those who love Him.*

JAMES 1:12 NLV

8

I will eat healthy meals.

Then God said, "Behold, I have given
you every plant yielding seed that
is on the surface of all the earth,
and every tree which has fruit yielding seed;
it shall be food for you; and to every beast
of the earth and to every bird of the sky
and to every thing that moves on the earth
which has life, I have given every green
plant for food"; and it was so.
God saw all that He had made, and
behold, it was very good. And there
was evening and there was morning,
the sixth day.

GENESIS 1:29–31 NASB

9

I will donate my free time to a worthwhile community activity.

"You've observed how godless rulers throw their weight around, how quickly a little power goes to their heads. It's not going to be that way with you. Whoever wants to be great must become a servant. Whoever wants to be first among you must be your slave. That is what the Son of Man has done: He came to serve, not be served—and then to give away his life in exchange for the many who are held hostage."
MATTHEW 20:25–28 MSG

10

I will relinquish a grudge.

*Therefore if you bring your gift
to the altar, and there remember
that your brother has something
against you, leave your gift there
before the altar, and go your way.
First be reconciled to your brother,
and then come and offer your gift.*

MATTHEW 5:23–24 NKJV

11

I won't worry about tomorrow.

"But seek first his kingdom and his righteousness, and all these things will be given to you as well. Therefore do not worry about tomorrow, for tomorrow will worry about itself. Each day has enough trouble of its own."
MATTHEW 6:33–34 NIV

12

I will take time to listen to the birds sing.

"Look at the birds in the sky. They do not plant seeds. They do not gather grain. They do not put grain into a building to keep. Yet your Father in heaven feeds them! Are you not more important than the birds?"

MATTHEW 6:26 NLV

13

I will be patient.

*Since God chose you to be the
holy people he loves,
you must clothe yourselves
with tenderhearted mercy, kindness,
humility, gentleness, and patience.
Make allowance for each other's faults,
and forgive anyone who offends you.
Remember, the Lord forgave you,
so you must forgive others.*

COLOSSIANS 3:12–13 NLT

14

I will show gratitude for acts of kindness toward me.

This gift you give not only helps Christians who are in need, but it also helps them give thanks to God. You are proving by this act of love what you are. They will give thanks to God for your gift to them and to others. This proves you obey the Good News of Christ. They will pray for you with great love because God has given you His loving-favor.

2 CORINTHIANS 9:12–14 NLV

15

I will read my Bible.

*With my whole heart have I sought thee:
O let me not wander from thy
commandments. Thy word have I
hid in mine heart, that I might not
sin against thee. Blessed art thou,
O Lord: teach me thy statutes.*
Psalm 119:10–12 kjv

16

I will set a good example
for others who may be
watching my actions.

*Follow my example, as I follow
the example of Christ.*
1 Corinthians 11:1 niv

17

I will find something to laugh about.

See, God will not turn away from
a man who is honest and faithful.
And He will not help those who do wrong.
He will yet make you laugh
and call out with joy.

JOB 8:20–21 NLV

18

I will pray for peace.

*Whoever of you loves life
and desires to see many good days,
keep your tongue from evil
and your lips from speaking lies.
Turn from evil and do good;
seek peace and pursue it.*
PSALM 34:12–14 NIV

19

I will be a person
of integrity.

*I know, my God, that you examine
our hearts and rejoice
when you find integrity there.*
1 CHRONICLES 29:17 NLT

101 RESOLUTIONS FOR THE NEW YEAR

20

I will be a mentor.

*And you yourself must be an example
to them by doing good works of every kind. Let
everything you do reflect the integrity
and seriousness of your teaching.
Teach the truth so that your teaching
can't be criticized. Then those who oppose
us will be ashamed and have nothing
bad to say about us.*

TITUS 2:7–8 NLT

21

I will put others before myself.

Do nothing out of selfish ambition
or vain conceit, but in humility
consider others better than yourselves.
Each of you should look not only
to your own interests, but also
to the interests of others.

Philippians 2:3–4 NIV

22

I will live in the present, not the past.

*Brethren, I do not regard myself
as having laid hold of it yet;
but one thing I do: forgetting what lies
behind and reaching forward to what
lies ahead, I press on toward the goal
for the prize of the upward call of
God in Christ Jesus.*

PHILIPPIANS 3:13–14 NASB

23

I will forgive myself.

For as the heavens are high above the earth, so great is His mercy toward those who fear Him; As far as the east is from the west, so far has He removed our transgressions from us. As a father pities his children, so the LORD pities those who fear Him.

PSALM 103:11–13 NKJV

24

I will be a friend
in deed.

This is love: not that we loved God,
but that he loved us and sent his
Son as an atoning sacrifice for our sins.
Dear friends, since God so loved us,
we also ought to love one another.
No one has ever seen God;
but if we love one another,
God lives in us and his love
is made complete in us.

1 JOHN 4:10–12 NIV

25

I will be less critical of others around me.

"Why do you look at the speck of sawdust in your brother's eye and pay no attention to the plank in your own eye? How can you say to your brother, 'Let me take the speck out of your eye,' when all the time there is a plank in your own eye? You hypocrite, first take the plank out of your own eye, and then you will see clearly to remove the speck from your brother's eye."

MATTHEW 7:3–5 NIV

26

I will be thankful
for what I have.

*In every thing give thanks: for this is the will
of God in Christ Jesus concerning you.*
1 THESSALONIANS 5:18 KJV

27

I will spend more time
in prayer for others
than for myself.

*For this reason also, since the day we heard
of it, we have not ceased to pray for you
and to ask that you may be filled with the
knowledge of His will in all spiritual wisdom
and understanding, so that you will walk in a
manner worthy of the Lord, to please Him in
all respects, bearing fruit in every good work
and increasing in the knowledge of God.*
COLOSSIANS 1:9–10 NASB

28

I will serve God.

"The man who loves his life will lose it,
while the man who hates his life
in this world will keep it for eternal life.
Whoever serves me must follow me;
and where I am, my servant also will be.
My Father will honor the one
who serves me."

John 12:25–26 niv

29

I will rejoice in the day that the Lord has made.

This was the LORD's doing;
It is marvelous in our eyes.
This is the day the LORD has made;
We will rejoice and be glad in it.
PSALM 118:23–24 NKJV

30

I will have hope
for the future.

For I know the thoughts that I think
toward you, says the Lord,
thoughts of peace and not of evil,
to give you a future and a hope.

JEREMIAH 29:11 NKJV

31

I will seek to know God better.

Know thou the God of thy father,
and serve him with a perfect heart
and with a willing mind:
for the LORD searcheth all hearts,
and understandeth all the imaginations
of the thoughts: if thou seek him,
he will be found of thee;
but if thou forsake him,
he will cast thee off for ever.

1 CHRONICLES 28:9 KJV

32

I will be a
cheerful giver.

*Remember this: Whoever sows
sparingly will also reap sparingly,
and whoever sows generously
will also reap generously.
Each man should give what
he has decided in his heart to give,
not reluctantly or under compulsion,
for God loves a cheerful giver.
And God is able to make
all grace abound to you,
so that in all things at all times,
having all that you need,
you will abound in every good work.*

2 CORINTHIANS 9:6–8 NIV

33

I will be fair.

*"Do not twist justice in
legal matters by favoring the poor
or being partial to the rich and powerful.
Always judge people fairly."*
LEVITICUS 19:15 NLT

34

I will be an encourager.

*I want them to be encouraged and knit
together by strong ties of love. I want them
to have complete confidence that they
understand God's mysterious plan, which
is Christ himself. In him lie hidden all the
treasures of wisdom and knowledge.*
COLOSSIANS 2:2–3 NLT

35

I will avoid procrastination.

*"We must keep on doing
the work of Him Who
sent Me while it is day.
Night is coming when no
man can work."*

JOHN 9:4 NLV

36

I will ponder God's perfect will for my life.

Do not conform any longer
to the pattern of this world,
but be transformed
by the renewing of your mind.
Then you will be able to test
and approve what God's will is—
his good, pleasing and perfect will.
ROMANS 12:2 NIV

37

I will be a
good neighbor.

*For all the law is fulfilled in one word,
even in this; Thou shalt love
thy neighbour as thyself.*
GALATIANS 5:14 KJV

38

I will put my confidence in God.

*This High Priest of ours understands
our weaknesses, for he faced all
of the same testings we do, yet he did
not sin. So let us come boldly to the
throne of our gracious God.
There we will receive his mercy,
and we will find grace to help us
when we need it most.*

<small>Hebrews 4:15–16 nlt</small>

39

I will treat others
with respect.

*Therefore encourage one another
and build each other up,
just as in fact you are doing.
Now we ask you, brothers, to respect
those who work hard among you,
who are over you in the Lord
and who admonish you. Hold them in
the highest regard in love because
of their work. Live in peace
with each other.*

1 Thessalonians 5:11–13 niv

40

I will do something that's outside my comfort zone.

"Have I not told you? Be strong
and have strength of heart!
Do not be afraid or lose faith.
For the Lord your God is with you
anywhere you go."
JOSHUA 1:9 NLV

41

I will not repeat yesterday's mistakes.

I applied my heart to what I observed
and learned a lesson from what I saw.
PROVERBS 24:32 NIV

42

I will take the initiative in standing up for righteousness.

*Pursue righteousness, godliness, faith,
love, perseverance and gentleness.
Fight the good fight of faith;
take hold of the eternal life
to which you were called, and you
made the good confession in the
presence of many witnesses.*

1 TIMOTHY 6:11–12 NASB

43

I will not allow
temporary frustrations
and disappointments
to derail me from achieving
my master goal.

*After beginning with the Spirit, are you
now trying to attain your goal
by human effort? Have you suffered
so much for nothing—if it really
was for nothing?*
GALATIANS 3:2–4 NIV

44

I will take a risk.

*Just then a woman who had hemorrhaged
for twelve years slipped in from
behind and lightly touched his robe.
She was thinking to herself, "If I can
just put a finger on his robe, I'll get well."
Jesus turned—caught her at it.
Then he reassured her: "Courage, daughter.
You took a risk of faith, and now
you're well." The woman was
well from then on.*
MATTHEW 9:20–22 MSG

45

I will praise a child for an accomplishment.

In that hour Jesus rejoiced in the Spirit and said, "I thank You, Father, Lord of heaven and earth, that You have hidden these things from the wise and prudent and revealed them to babes. Even so, Father, for so it seemed good in Your sight."
LUKE 10:21 NKJV

46

I will smile.

They longed for me to speak
as people long for rain. They drank
my words like a refreshing spring rain.
When they were discouraged,
I smiled at them. My look of approval
was precious to them.
Like a chief, I told them what to do.
I lived like a king among his troops
and comforted those who mourned.

JOB 29:23–25 NLT

47

I will look for the good in others.

The honor of good people will lead them, but those who hurt others will be destroyed by their own false ways.

PROVERBS 11:3 NLV

48

I will simplify my life by decreasing my debt.

Don't run up debts, except for the huge debt of love you owe each other.
ROMANS 13:8 MSG

49

I will lean on God's strength.

Trust in the LORD with all thine heart; and lean not unto thine own understanding. In all thy ways acknowledge him, and he shall direct thy paths.
PROVERBS 3:5–6 KJV

50

I will share the joy of answered prayer.

*The LORD is far from the wicked,
but he hears the prayer
of the righteous.*
PROVERBS 15:29 NLT

51

I will say "I love you" more often.

You've captured my heart, dear friend.
You looked at me, and I fell in love.
One look my way and I was hopelessly in love!
How beautiful your love, dear, dear friend—
far more pleasing than a fine, rare wine,
your fragrance more exotic than select spices.
The kisses of your lips are honey,
my love, every syllable you speak a
delicacy to savor.
SONG OF SOLOMON 4:9–11 MSG

52

I will say grace
in a restaurant.

*I am not ashamed of the Good News.
It is the power of God. It is the
way He saves men from the
punishment of their sins if they
put their trust in Him.*

ROMANS 1:16 NLV

53

I will be thrifty.

*Now therefore, thus says the Lord
of hosts, "Consider your ways!
You have sown much, but harvest little;
you eat, but there is not enough
to be satisfied; you drink, but there
is not enough to become drunk;
you put on clothing, but no one is
warm enough; and he who earns,
earns wages to put into a
purse with holes."*

Haggai 1:5–6 nasb

54

I will avoid impropriety.

Be imitators of God, therefore, as dearly loved children and live a life of love, just as Christ loved us and gave himself up for us as a fragrant offering and sacrifice to God.
But among you there must not be even a hint of sexual immorality, or of any kind of impurity, or of greed, because these are improper for God's holy people. Nor should there be obscenity, foolish talk or coarse joking, which are out of place, but rather thanksgiving.
For of this you can be sure:
No immoral, impure or greedy person— such a man is an idolater—has any inheritance in the kingdom of Christ and of God.

Ephesians 5:1–5 niv

55

I will live a life
pleasing to God.

*For the kingdom of God is not meat
and drink; but righteousness, and peace,
and joy in the Holy Ghost. For he that
in these things serveth Christ is acceptable
to God, and approved of men.*
ROMANS 14:17–18 KJV

56

I will count my blessings instead of my burdens.

O my soul, bless GOD. From head to toe,
I'll bless his holy name!
O my soul, bless GOD, don't forget
a single blessing!
He forgives your sins—every one.
He heals your diseases—every one.
He redeems you from hell—saves your life!
He crowns you with love and mercy—
a paradise crown.
He wraps you in goodness—
beauty eternal.
He renews your youth—you're always
young in his presence.

PSALM 103:1–5 MSG

57

I will set my standards
a little higher.

*As for me, may I never boast
about anything except the cross of our
Lord Jesus Christ. Because of that cross,
my interest in this world has been
crucified, and the world's interest
in me has also died. It doesn't matter
whether we have been circumcised or not.
What counts is whether we have been
transformed into a new creation.
May God's peace and mercy be upon
all who live by this principle;
they are the new people of God.*
GALATIANS 6:14–16 NLT

58

I will ask God to give me
a job to do for Him, and
then will follow through.

*And now, O Israel, what does the Lord
your God ask of you but to fear the
Lord your God, to walk in all his ways,
to love him, to serve the Lord your God
with all your heart and with all your soul,
and to observe the Lord's commands
and decrees that I am giving you
today for your own good?*
DEUTERONOMY 10:12–13 NIV

59

I will do my
best.

*But according to His promise
we are looking for new heavens
and a new earth, in which righteousness
dwells. Therefore, beloved, since you
look for these things, be diligent to be
found by Him in peace,
spotless and blameless.*

2 PETER 3:13–14 NASB

60

I will spend more time on my knees in prayer.

God's Word is an indispensable weapon. In the same way, prayer is essential in this ongoing warfare. Pray hard and long. Pray for your brothers and sisters. Keep your eyes open. Keep each other's spirits up so that no one falls behind or drops out.
EPHESIANS 6:17–18 MSG

61

I will enjoy
life's spontaneity.

*Here's my concern: that you care for
God's flock with all the diligence of a shepherd.
Not because you have to, but because you
want to please God. Not calculating what
you can get out of it, but acting spontaneously.
Not bossily telling others what to do, but
tenderly showing them the way.*

1 PETER 5:2–3 MSG

62

I will mean what I say, and say what I mean.

Let me say it again. Have nothing to do with foolish talk and those who want to argue. It can only lead to trouble.

2 TIMOTHY 2:23 NLV

63

I will plant the seed of hope in someone whose garden of life is full of weeds.

Behold, thou hast instructed many, and thou hast strengthened the weak hands. Thy words have upholden him that was falling, and thou hast strengthened the feeble knees.

JOB 4:3–4 KJV

64

I will say no to a request when I am already overextended.

We are no longer to be children, tossed here and there by waves and carried about by every wind of doctrine, by the trickery of men, by craftiness in deceitful scheming; but speaking the truth in love, we are to grow up in all aspects into Him who is the head, even Christ.

Ephesians 4:14–15 nasb

65

I will choose to be joyful.

Our mouths were filled with laughter,
our tongues with songs of joy.
Then it was said among the nations,
"The Lord has done great things for them."
The Lord has done great things for us,
and we are filled with joy.

Psalm 126:2–3 niv

66

I will recognize unwanted interruptions as opportunities for ministry rather than reasons for frustration.

Be wise in the way you act toward outsiders; make the most of every opportunity.
COLOSSIANS 4:5 NIV

67

I will use my minutes wisely.

Plant your seed in the morning and keep busy all afternoon, for you don't know if profit will come from one activity or another—or maybe both.
ECCLESIASTES 11:6 NLT

68

I will chase away unwholesome thoughts.

*For God did not call us to uncleanness,
but in holiness. Therefore he who rejects
this does not reject man, but God, who
has also given us His Holy Spirit.*

1 Thessalonians 4:7–8 NKJV

69

I will make injustice
my adversary.

"Is this not the fast which I choose,
to loosen the bonds of wickedness,
to undo the bands of the yoke,
and to let the oppressed go free
and break every yoke?"
ISAIAH 58:6 NASB

70

I will spread good news.

So they set out and went from village
to village, preaching the gospel and
healing people everywhere.
LUKE 9:6 NIV

101 RESOLUTIONS FOR THE NEW YEAR

71

I will deny the urge to burst someone's bubble.

Don't use foul or abusive language.
Let everything you say be good and helpful,
so that your words will be an encouragement
to those who hear them.

Ephesians 4:29 nlt

101 RESOLUTIONS FOR THE NEW YEAR

72

I will overcome timidity and speak up for righteousness.

"Now, Lord, consider their threats and enable your servants to speak your word with great boldness."
ACTS 4:29 NIV

73

I will memorize
scripture.

*Fix these words of mine in your hearts
and minds; tie them as symbols on your
hands and bind them on your foreheads.
Teach them to your children, talking
about them when you sit at home
and when you walk along the road,
when you lie down and when you get up.
Write them on the doorframes of
your houses and on your gates, so that
your days and the days of your children
may be many in the land that the LORD
swore to give your forefathers, as many
as the days that the heavens
are above the earth.*

DEUTERONOMY 11:18–21 NIV

101 RESOLUTIONS FOR THE NEW YEAR

74

I will leave vengeance
in the Lord's hands.

Live peaceably with all men.
Dearly beloved, avenge not yourselves,
but rather give place unto wrath:
for it is written, Vengeance is mine;
I will repay, saith the Lord.
Therefore if thine enemy hunger, feed him;
if he thirst, give him drink: for in so doing
thou shalt heap coals of fire on his head.
ROMANS 12:18–20 KJV

75

I will practice mercy.

Talk and act like a person expecting to be judged by the Rule that sets us free. For if you refuse to act kindly, you can hardly expect to be treated kindly. Kind mercy wins over harsh judgment every time.

JAMES 2:12–13 MSG

76

I will do a good deed in secret.

But when you give to someone in need, don't let your left hand know what your right hand is doing. Give your gifts in private, and your Father, who sees everything, will reward you.

Matthew 6:3–4 NLT

77

I will carry someone else's burden.

Carry each other's burdens, and in this way you will fulfill the law of Christ.
GALATIANS 6:2 NIV

78

I will not be intimidated by others.

"Keep it up, and don't let anyone intimidate or silence you. No matter what happens, I'm with you and no one is going to be able to hurt you."
ACTS 18:9 MSG

79

I will be a better money manager.

Some good comes from all work.
Nothing but talk leads only to being poor.
What the wise receive is their riches, but
fools are known by their foolish ways.
PROVERBS 14:23–24 NLV

101 RESOLUTIONS FOR THE NEW YEAR

80

I will be a proper steward of all that God has entrusted to me.

For everyone to whom much is given,
from him much will be required;
and to whom much has been committed,
of him they will ask the more.
LUKE 12:48 NKJV

81

I will return a borrowed item—with interest.

*The wicked borroweth, and payeth
not again: but the righteous
sheweth mercy, and giveth.*
PSALM 37:21 KJV

82

I will awaken with a thankful heart.

Your thoughts—how rare, how beautiful!
God, I'll never comprehend them!
I couldn't even begin to count them—
any more than I could count the
sand of the sea.
Oh, let me rise in the morning
and live always with you!

PSALM 139:17–18 MSG

83

I will believe that
God will give me the
desires of my heart.

*May he grant your heart's desires
and make all your plans succeed.*

Psalm 20:4 nlt

101
RESOLUTIONS FOR THE NEW YEAR

84

I will strive to meet
the potential that God
had in mind when
He created me.

And he died for all, that those who live
should no longer live for themselves
but for him who died for them and was
raised again. So from now on we regard
no one from a worldly point of view.
Though we once regarded Christ in this
way, we do so no longer. Therefore, if
anyone is in Christ, he is a new creation;
the old has gone, the new has come!

2 CORINTHIANS 5:15–17 NIV

85

I will back up my convictions with appropriate actions.

If anyone has material possessions and sees his brother in need but has no pity on him, how can the love of God be in him? Dear children, let us not love with words or tongue but with actions and in truth. This then is how we know that we belong to the truth, and how we set our hearts at rest in his presence.

1 John 3:17–19 niv

101 RESOLUTIONS FOR THE NEW YEAR

86

I will erase the memory of—but not the lessons from—past errors.

So let us leave the first things you need to know about Christ. Let us go on to the teaching that full-grown Christians should understand. We do not need to teach these first truths again. You already know that you must be sorry for your sins and turn from them. You know that you must have faith in God.

Hebrews 6:1 NLV

87

I will obey
God's laws.

*"Teacher, which is the greatest
commandment in the Law?"
Jesus replied: " 'Love the Lord your God
with all your heart and with all your
soul and with all your mind.' This is the
first and greatest commandment.
And the second is like it: 'Love your
neighbor as yourself.' All the Law
and the Prophets hang on these
two commandments."*

MATTHEW 22:36–40 NIV

88

I will stitch up small
tears in relationships before
they become major ones.

*Be ye angry, and sin not: let not the
sun go down upon your wrath:
Neither give place to the devil.*
Ephesians 4:26–27 KJV

89

I will be a friend to the friendless.

"Then the righteous will answer Him, 'Lord, when did we see You hungry, and feed You, or thirsty, and give You something to drink? And when did we see You a stranger, and invite You in, or naked, and clothe You? When did we see You sick, or in prison, and come to You?' The King will answer and say to them, 'Truly I say to you, to the extent that you did it to one of these brothers of Mine, even the least of them, you did it to Me.'"
MATTHEW 25:37–40 NASB

90

I will open my home to others.

Be joyful in hope, patient in affliction, faithful in prayer. Share with God's people who are in need. Practice hospitality.
ROMANS 12:12–13 NIV

91

I will cover my
days with prayer.

*"Ask, and what you are asking for will
be given to you. Look, and what you are
looking for you will find. Knock, and the
door you are knocking on will be opened
to you. Everyone who asks receives what
he asks for. Everyone who looks finds
what he is looking for. Everyone who
knocks has the door opened to him."*
MATTHEW 7:7–8 NLV

92

I will expect the best to happen instead of imagining the worst.

There's more to come: We continue to shout our praise even when we're hemmed in with troubles, because we know how troubles can develop passionate patience in us, and how that patience in turn forges the tempered steel of virtue, keeping us alert for whatever God will do next. In alert expectancy such as this, we're never left feeling shortchanged. Quite the contrary—we can't round up enough containers to hold everything God generously pours into our lives through the Holy Spirit!

ROMANS 5:3–5 MSG

93

I will snub
no one.

*"Do not insult the deaf or cause the blind to
stumble. You must fear your God; I am
the LORD. Do not twist justice in legal
matters by favoring the poor or being partial
to the rich and powerful. Always judge
people fairly. Do not spread slanderous
gossip among your people. Do not stand
idly by when your neighbor's life is threatened.
I am the LORD."*

LEVITICUS 19:14–16 NLT

94

I will dissolve misunderstandings.

*If any of you has a dispute with another,
dare he take it before the ungodly for
judgment instead of before the saints?
Do you not know that the saints will judge
the world? And if you are to judge the world,
are you not competent to judge trivial cases?
Do you not know that we will judge angels?
How much more the things of this life!*
1 CORINTHIANS 6:1–3 NIV

95

I will persevere.

*Cast not away therefore your confidence,
which hath great recompence of reward.
For ye have need of patience, that, after ye
have done the will of God, ye might receive
the promise. For yet a little while, and he that
shall come will come, and will not tarry.*

HEBREWS 10:35–37 KJV

96

I will face the person in the mirror with enthusiasm.

My dear children, let's not just talk about love; let's practice real love. This is the only way we'll know we're living truly, living in God's reality. It's also the way to shut down debilitating self-criticism, even when there is something to it. For God is greater than our worried hearts and knows more about us than we do ourselves.

1 John 3:18–20 msg

97

I will forgive
and forget.

*A man's understanding makes him slow
to anger. It is to his honor to forgive
and forget a wrong done to him.*
PROVERBS 19:11 NLV

98

I will play more.

*But he's already made it plain how to live,
what to do, what GOD is looking for in men
and women. It's quite simple: Do what
is fair and just to your neighbor,
be compassionate and loyal in your love,
and don't take yourself too seriously—
take God seriously.*

MICAH 6:8 MSG

99

I will make more time for my family.

"Go home to your family and tell them how much the Lord has done for you, and how he has had mercy on you."

Mark 5:19 NIV

100

I will make a difference in the world.

"I've come to start a fire on this earth—how I wish it were blazing right now! I've come to change everything, turn everything rightside up—how I long for it to be finished! Do you think I came to smooth things over and make everything nice? Not so. I've come to disrupt and confront!

LUKE 12:49–51 MSG

101

I will share a laugh with someone in need of a little joy.

Our mouths were filled with laughter, our tongues with songs of joy. Then it was said among the nations, "The LORD has done great things for them."
PSALM 126:2 NIV